Independence Day

by Susan Hood
✶
illustrated by
Lori McElrath Eslick

Scott Foresman

Editorial Offices: Glenview, Illinois • New York, New York
Sales Offices: Reading, Massachusetts • Duluth, Georgia
Glenview, Illinois • Carrollton, Texas • Menlo Park, California

"Will we still have the family baseball game this year?" asked Clare. "The Fourth of July won't be the same without grounders, outs, and home runs."

"We will just have to wait and see," said Clare's mom with a sigh. "It will depend on how Grandpa Teddy is doing."

Clare's grandfather had had a stroke. He was home from the hospital. But he just wasn't the same.

Grandpa Teddy had been a great baseball player. Now he had to sit in a wheelchair. He could only move his right arm.

Clare's mom tried to pretend that things would be all right. But Clare saw the circles under her eyes. She knew she was worried. Would things ever be all right again?

In the past, the Wades had always held a big family reunion on the Fourth of July. Everyone came. There was Grandma Rose and Grandpa Teddy, along with aunts, uncles, and cousins from out of town.

It was a family tradition to play baseball at the reunion. Every year, Clare's grandparents chose the teams and handed out the official uniforms—T-shirts! The teams were called Rose's Buds and Teddy's Bears. But what would happen this year with Grandpa so sick?

The Fourth of July arrived. Surprise! Everyone came, just as they always did. And Grandma Rose and Grandpa Teddy handed out T-shirts. Clare was thrilled.

Grandma picked Clare's brother Rick for her team. "Oh, Rick," taunted Clare's cousin, "you'll be such a pretty Rose Bud!"

Grandpa handed Clare a Teddy's Bears T-shirt. "Thanks, Grandpa," she said. "Who is going to play for you?"

"I AM!" shouted Grandpa gruffly.

"Won't that be too dangerous for Grandpa?" Clare said to herself.

Clare's dad wheeled Grandpa across the
baseball diamond. He was going to play outfield.

"Are you sure he's okay?" asked Clare's
mom when her dad returned.

"This is important to him," said Clare's dad.
"He's far out in the outfield. He'll be perfectly
safe. Let him feel as if he is part of the game.
After all, it is Independence Day. Now let's
play ball!"

Soon it was the Bears' turn up at bat. Clare stepped up to the plate first. The pitch was long and low. Clare swung hard. Strike!

Clare's uncle pitched again. This time, Clare hit a grounder to second base and ran to first. Safe!

"Good girl!" shouted Grandpa.

Clare smiled.

Clare's sister smashed the ball and brought Clare home. By the bottom of the inning, the Bears were ahead 2–0!

Rose's Buds stepped up to bat. Clare's cousin Bill hit a grounder to third base. He ran to second. Clare's dad hit a home run. Then Clare's Aunt Lucy scored a run. Soon the score was Bears 2, Buds 3.

By the ninth inning, the Bears were one run ahead. It was Bears 12, Buds 11. But Rose's Buds had one more turn at bat. Anything could happen!

First, Cousin Nick struck out. Then Cousin Annie was tagged at third base. Two outs! But Clare's dad—Slugger Sam—was up. Would he hit another home run? Would the Buds tie the score? Clare's dad stepped up to the plate.

The pitch came. Slam! The ball whizzed
up, up, and up. It soared far across the
baseball diamond, high above Grandpa
in his wheelchair.

Grandpa raised his glove in the air.
He was ready.

"No one could catch that!" taunted Clare's cousin. "Slugger Sam is going to get us another home run."

"Don't be so sure," said Clare, although she knew it was true. After Grandpa's stroke, how could he catch that ball?

Smack! The ball dropped straight down
into Grandpa Teddy's glove. Dad was out!
Thanks to Grandpa Teddy, Teddy's Bears won
the game!

"Grandpa Teddy, you're the best!"
said Clare.

"You always were," said Grandma Rose
to her husband. "And you always will be!"

Grandpa Teddy beamed at his wife and
winked at Clare. "Enough of this mushy stuff,"
he said. "How about another game?"